NOT YET IN HEAVEN

MORE INTIMATE HAIKU

MICHAEL J. LEE

First Edition 2021

ISBN 978-1-77630-220-8 (eBook)

ISBN 978-1-77630-221-5 (Print)

www.michaeljlee.com

www.beyondheads.com

Cover and interior crafted with love by the team at:
www.myebook.online

Contents

Poet's Preface

The haiku is defined numerically by the number of syllables in each of its three lines, so there's a basic numerical structure to all haiku. I find myself counting in my mind or on my hands as I check that each haiku is correct in terms of the number of its syllables per line. It's like playing a miniature piano which only has 17 keys. And, so, it's true that the music of haiku is composed of very few notes. It's the briefest of all poetic forms. We are dealing with mere particles of art.

Its saving grace is probably that life is made up of moments and matter is made up of atoms. Reality is founded on the small and the brief. It's microscopic. The game, then, isn't just a matter of numbers, hitting the right number of keys in the right order. It's about a truth the Impressionists understood so well: let's capture the particles of light as they flicker on leaves in the breeze, or on the rippling surfaces of lakes, ponds and oceans. Or let's paint the varied skin tones of a face's expression in a portrait.

Haiku, too, are only impressions of the world, or the reflections of an insight as it passes through the mind, or the

———————

statement of a single idea. They encapsulate single thoughts and single experiences.

The title *Not Yet in Heaven* reflects the idea of being an aspiring person and idealist at heart in a flawed world, yet one touched by glory. Accordingly, many haiku in the volume articulate the sense of being in the midst of a process of seeking fulfilment, of finding different kinds of momentary peace. If we are "not yet in heaven", how precious is hope itself!

Michael J. Lee

Cape Town

2021

1. Connect

Feel God in the light,
in the heat: in the slow peace
of a new morning.

2. Pool

Calm pool within me:
each act, or thought, sends ripples
in perfect circles.

3. On this day

Opportunities:
to show the power of love,
or waste history.

4. Airborne

Bird flying so high,
you're so vital in the sky;
teach me your secrets.

5. Pillars

Pillars of the Earth
uphold the world constantly:
a living support.

6. Timepiece

I heard the click, tick
of the old clock, telling me
it's not over yet.

———————

7. One day

One day when love rules
we'll all be our happiest,
letting all pain go.

8. Blue

Shiny, cracked window,
magnetic sun pours out blue:
an unbroken day.

9. Bright night

Stars of dark, blue night,
and high clouds afloat in space,
flood midnight's late peace.

10.   *Live wired*

Neurons, like networks
of power lines, pulse with life:
signals of purpose.

11.   *Energetic*

My breathing cells burn
air and food in energy
flowing into me.

12.   *Free now*

Let me be at peace,
let me see clearly and true
that all life is free.

13. *It's a good day*

Today's a good day;
sunlight after night showers:
Earth, now we're ready.

14. *Transition*

Spring's stuttering start
dissolves into profusion:
gardens are smiling.

15. *Respect*

Respect is like air
fed into our breath and blood,
waking us to life.

16.   Love's voice

What would Love say here,
what would Love say now to us?
"I am like the Sun."

17.   Dawn bird

"Thank you, we are safe,
thank you, we're happy and free,"
chirps a bird at dawn.

18.   Alive in love

Love breathes into life
its soul, filling the vacuum
to overflowing.

19.   She and me

XX and XY
are the only reasons why…
she's she and I'm me.

20.   Renewal

Press Reset and pause.
Life is God's, so I pray for
goodness to prevail.

21.   Shimmer of sunshine

Everything seems right
in late summer day sunlight:
enough heat for all.

22. Sunbird

Spring must be near,
a ruby red blossom brings
a green sunbird here.

23. Beach scene

First published in *Stanzas* poetry magazine

Such skies, sea and dunes!
Gaze into nature's mirror
to see who you are.

24. Not yet done

I'm not finished yet.
I might walk on the bright moon.
Barriers will break.

25. *Lizard*

Bathed in morning sun,
a lizard on a rock rests,
warming head and blood.

26. *On joy*

Love's the friend of joy:
do little acts with much love
to set your joy free.

27. *The gift (i)*

I received a gift.
Inside was incredible:
the gift was a choice.

28. The gift (ii)

My life is a gift.
What can I best do with it
to honour its worth?

29. The gift (iii)

The gift deserves care.
It's outside, it's inside me;
it's my destiny.

30. Robin redbreast

A small robin hops
in hope in cold, morning gloom,
Spring still in the womb.

31. *All lined up*

The Sun is as far
from the Moon as it's bigger:
a perfect eclipse.

32. *Mountain city*

I live with the world:
kaleidoscopic Cape Town,
friend of the Mountain.

33. *The kingdom within...*

I can't see or feel
what's ephemera or real
if my heart won't heal.

34. Open ground

A sea of shanties
soon materialised there:
the poor are with us.

35. Stateless

Heaven's a country
on high for humanity:
no cops required.

36. Atmosphere

Two billion years
of bacteria breathing
created Earth's breath.

37.   *Heal*

When my soul's in pain
and when your soul is hurting,
let's heal each other.

38.   *Words*

My words heal or hurt,
build or break, sow or sever:
help me to choose well.

39.   *The Beatles*

Timeless songs belong
to anyone, like the air:
where your sound was born.

40.   *Peaceful*

Nothing is perfect,
no one is above reproach:
peace is perfection...

41.   *Switch*

Set your dial to Love.
Flip your soul's switch to goodness.
Morning comes each day.

42.   *A balanced day*

Not too much to do,
not too little for one day:
it'll be just fine.

43. *In a pandemic*

This cataclysm
will pass; progress is precious:
a world born again.

44. *Time imprints*

Chiselled by my past,
I shape and carve my future:
creations of time.

45. *Whole love*

Let love become whole,
in my soul, out in the world:
soothing wrongs and hurts.

46. Vangelis

Keyboard maestro,
I salute the deep beauty
of soaring soundscapes.

47. Who?

Who knows I am here...
placed into the world under
everlasting light.

48. Thankfulness

Thanksgiving cleanses
my whole body, mind and soul:
a flood of goodness.

49.   One morning walk

Be mindful of light,
thankful for breathing and strength,
happy just to be.

50.   Creative

Explosive life force,
fountainhead of creation:
my art of birth pains.

51.   Failed

Failure isn't death.
Don't stop creating culture.
Even sparrows strive!

52. *Living web*

The planet's green leaves
capture sunny energy
grounding the food web.

53. *Tears*

Down my face tears
travelled miles and miles in me
from a well of sighs.

54. *Guide*

I call God my Guide,
creating laws of nature
to steer journeys.

55. Rule of love

Love has ruled my heart,
forgiving sins and sinners,
transforming failures.

56. Organic Lego™

Cells make tissues and
tissues form organs, muscles
and bones: who we are.

57. A reorientation

Where did my time fly?
Where did my destiny go?
I face my future.

58. *All well...*

Let us all be well,
as well as the living cells
breathing within us.

59. *Empires of the old*

Fading worlds bully
younger worlds growing stronger:
old patriarchies.

60. *Being*

I am a being,
cocooned in all creation:
ready for rebirths.

61.   Answered

I needed nurture.
I searched the Mind of Nature:
God gave an answer.

62.   Winter's end

Give life fresh meaning,
as Winter took everything;
kind Spring, breathe on us.

63.   Solved

No fear's too great,
in my adventure of days,
to beat energy.

64.   Time map

No random journey
is this life charted by Time,
gifted with seasons.

65.   The truth twister

The man-dragon breathes
fire of populism,
hate and deception.

66.   More light

My heart needs more light
to see the pain of others,
to know what Love is.

67.   Quadruple troubles

Storm surges flood homes,
bush fires rage, riots roar,
as infections soar.

68.   Direction

We can be convinced,
but wrong, resolute but lost:
follow the sun's path.

69.   Markets

Sell no soul to stocks,
or the market's ghostly grip
will lead you astray.

70.   *Throne*

Throne of energy
fills up the sky with glory,
bursting with colour.

71.   *Epitaph for a president*

His morality
is his egomania:
"Magnify my brand."

72.   *A higher goodness*

Let goodness win, Lord,
not mine, or ours, but yours:
your glory above.

73.   *Power of love*

Wake up with the light.
Forgive all your enemies:
let love heal our world.

74.   *Loneliness*

The loneliest place
is the heart in need of love...
when there is no love.

75.   *Timed*

Now time is fading.
I wish I'd been much kinder.
Let me end stronger.

76.   *Breathe*

I breathe air, I eat:
life-energy flows in me,
renewing living.

77.   *Politics and peace*

Polarisation
is where politics exists:
who will bring us peace?

78.   *Good Samaritans*

A smile can heal hurts,
empathy may renew hope:
light is warm and bright.

79.   My progress

Stumbling, falling man,
I triumph in tiny steps,
let light heal my mind.

80.   Guys

Guys can like flowers
in God's universe of peace:
loving living things.

81.   Subtlety

Subtle is the touch,
lightly is the style of grace:
art dances in time.

82.   Head space

My head needs healing
to trust humans as my own:
or I face a trap.

83.   Bible

I love my Bible,
an old Owner's Manual
for safe use of life.

84.   A night scene

The night is quiet
as a closed grand piano
yearning to be played.

85.   Factory

I'm a factory.
Cells are workers building me,
constructing being.

86.   Serving

Serve with dignity,
love with grace, live with purpose:
giving away cares.

87.   Ageing

Ageing is a fate
almost as bad as death is,
until we fight back.

88. *Face the front*

I face forward, or
vanish into the long night:
the path never ends.

89. *My biome*

South of Africa,
my biome, my breathing space:
what builds her, builds me.

90. *Night sky*

Deep beyond frail clouds,
sunlight flashes off the moon:
sign of tomorrow.

91.   *Diary of a daisy*

Barberton daisies:
full, open, orange faces:
children of the suns.

92.   *Dark night*

Sleep is light, thoughts churn,
dark and angry is the world;
bring peace from on high.

93.   *Bird of youth*

So! Beautiful bird,
so high, so free in the sky:
teach me of your youth.

94.   *Flame of vitality*

All the good music,
movies, friends, fun, love, sex, sport,
kept my flame burning.

95.   *Believe bigger*

Trouble is brewing,
rapidly bubbling over:
I pray for more faith.

96.   *A day in the city*

An arc of colours
dipped into the city bowl
its hazy dazzle.

97.   Crying

I cry for my land,
for our poor, hungry ones;
rainbows born again.

98.   Undefeated

The bully can thrive
if the victims stay quiet,
or never fight back.

99.   Flames

Like flames in fire
energy feeds on food's fuel
in burning bodies.

100. Thinking about thinking

Think small to think big.
Cells. Atoms. Elements. Dust.
Facts trump opinions.

101. Rain in Africa

Africa's rain, bless
our sky and soil, roots and seeds:
heal our hunger.

102. Nocturnal glow

Grey-blue night sky glows;
tonight, the moon is golden:
making us all rich.

103. Solutions

Out-think the problem
to find a new solution:
use cause-and-effect.

104. Things will be fine

Sow God's love wider
and lift his good name higher:
let true power grow.

105. Spring song

For whom does Spring bloom,
but for songbirds and new buds
and those who can hope?

106. *The emergence*

We emerged in fields,
friends of trees, plants, beasts and birds;
look back in wonder.

107. *Loyal love*

God's loyal love gives
the hope you need to succeed;
feel faith flowing free.

108. *Reflections*

My ego and me:
narcissisms everywhere:
empty reflections.

109. Catharsis

Cry for a flawed world,
weep for a broken system,
pray for better days.

110. A summer evening

A breeze lifts the leaves
as Orion's Belt flickers:
freshness fills the air.

111. Nihilism

Don't be infected
by nihilistic Nietzsche
or life-negation.

112.   *Stress relief*

Stop stress reaching you
to strangle you from inside:
rest, relax, renew!

113.   *Oxygenated*

I give thanks today
to Mr and Mrs Plant
for life's oxygen.

114.   *Awakening*

Memories in dreams
faded at dawn in the songs.
And birds loved the morn.

115.   *Through any dark times*

Thank you for goodness,
thank you for your provision
and all promises.

116.   *What persists*

I survived my past,
all around me, life looks fine:
God rules tomorrow.

117.   *Strong*

No worry, no doubt,
no fear or cowering:
be humble, but bold.

118.   A rare love

Hate set at default,
love became rare, uncommon:
but love never dies.

119.   A powerful love

God's love shall not fail.
It enfolds my family,
wrapping us in grace.

120.   X folks

They are X people:
low-empathy egotists,
recklessly selfish.

121. *Y folks*

They are Yes people
who never exploit others:
building better worlds.

122. *Peace*

Peace is a cool pool,
a deep, clear aquifer:
overflowing springs.

123. *Frond*

A palm frond floated,
but I heard no wind, just wings
whooshing overhead.

124. *West coast scene (i)*

First published in *Stanzas* poetry magazine

The shore's rushing hush
rustles across fynbos veld:
stirring swooping birds.

125. *West coast scene (ii)*

First published in *Stanzas* poetry magazine

Social weavers' huts
sway from fronds waving freely
beside the wild sea.

126. *West coast scene (iii)*

First published in *Stanzas* poetry magazine

Squeaky caws of gulls
pierce the salty air near dunes;
waves surf sand and shells.

---

127. *Predetermined*

It's written in genes
and in DNA, not stars:
genomic futures.

128. *Where honour belongs*

All honour is God's,
taking no glory for me;
let his suns shine on.

129. *Union*

Secret processes
of life's mystery bind us:
atom to atom.

130. *Greatest show*

Nature is better
than a movie or painting:
spectacular truths.

131. *Co-ordinates*

Fixed in time and space,
like an arrow follows laws,
I move with purpose.

132. *A still morning*

Knife-sharp light pierces
the strong, expectant garden
in bright synthesis.

133. *Veld (i)*

The veld's green ocean
flickers with wings on the wind:
a whistling in evening.

134. *Veld (ii)*

Birds predominate
in the undisturbed reserve,
sniffing fynbos scents.

135. *Veld (iii)*

I love the still veld,
it lets me be, or walk free,
breathing easily.

136. *Good things*

For every good thing
I give thanks and praise my God,
while my days persist.

137. *A different pace*

In the slow country
I find new peace in its pace:
timeless fields and sea.

138. *Provided*

God gives what I need:
daylight, starlight and moonlight
for seeing my way.

139. Poor petals

Poverty's petals
bloom in hope that can't be cheap:
promise of progress.

140. Skywards

Unclench fisted hands,
stop hating and start loving:
face skywards for light.

141. Strong

Heal me strong and whole,
heal the world of hurts and hate,
rising together.

142. *Blue sky days*

I live for blue skies,
when the world's face is smiling
in long, summer days.

143. *Reality check*

What seems, is, will be;
all dissolves into essence;
only love prevails.

144. *Positivity*

What is positive
and right is good for my soul:
goodness finds me well.

145. Protection

Dipolar planet...
blue magnetospheric world
a-buzz with living.

146. Thanksgiving

Thank you, God of life:
giving us so much goodness,
easing our burdens.

147. Times

What seems, is a dream,
what has been, will be again:
believing is real.

148. Scones

My wife baked her scones
as the sun baked a new day
for my hungry mouth.

149. Prospects

Let love be bolder,
let forgiveness be stronger,
let hope glow brighter.

150. Rays

Sun tips the tree tops,
a glow overflows in blue:
two cats mesmerised.

151.   Fathers?

What good can be done
by fathers who can't show love,
who can't hold a hand?

152.   Christ

He came for us all,
to bind the broken-hearted,
to free us from guilt.

153.   Religious ideology

Denominations.
We must find what unites us.
No more wars of words.

154. Reactionary

Reactionary.
Tempted by my fate to hate,
I seek redemption.

155. Why be positive?

Positivity
is good for our thoughts and hearts.
It protects our hopes.

156. Reborn

Over and over,
let our beliefs be reborn,
for a stronger mind.

157. Knowledge

A beautiful word
is "knowable": to know truth.
Knowing sets us free.

158. First morning

This orange daisy
craves sunshine to be made whole
in spring's first morning.

159. Daily goal

I get up each day...
and it's about being loved,
then loving God back.

160.   *The angry beggar's gob*

At the traffic light,
he spat on my closed window:
wind swabbed bitterness.

161.   *Self-affirmation*

I'm not the loser
they all wanted me to be.
Call me: child of God.

162.   *In praise of Desiderata*

I can set my watch
by Desiderata's themes:
for all times of life.

———

163. *Plea for science*

Plain science, set free
from vain, jaw-breaking jargon,
can power progress.

164. *More thanksgiving*

Thank you for today,
thank you for my tomorrow:
I cradle my time.

165. *Greatest*

The greatest of all
is a God who creates breath:
source of truth and life.

166. *Peace arrived*

Don't speak; peace is here.
It tells us not to fear.
It states: "All is well".

167. *Kirstenbosch*

Early summer day
bathes canopies in stillness:
we breathe in greenness.

168. *Accountancy*

Pay for night shelters,
pay for food banks, hospitals:
love is expensive.

169.   Ideal world

In my ideal world,
all get the kiss of success:
hard work rewarded.

170.   A deep sleep

A sleep of healing
smothered me in peacefulness:
I awoke stronger.

171.   Peas in a pod

"Who am I?" I ask.
I'm 24,000 genes
but call me Michael.

172. *Postures*

Posturing bullies,
showboating in media,
weave their illusions.

173. *Web*

The food web was planned,
water and sunlight feeding
power into life.

174. *The forces*

The strong nuclear force
binds our core, as gravity
holds planets in place.

175.   *A plea for logic*

Not superstition,
neither fragments of knowledge,
can build our future.

176.   *Balance of forces*

The balance is good:
why not fight for the cosmos?
The forces free us.

177.   *A marriage union*

Loving made us whole,
coals fading into starlight:
pure forgetfulness.

178.   The glory

If I have glory,
how can I love God's glory?
It is peace I serve.

179.   Wisdom

God founded wisdom:
families of galaxies,
cycles of seasons.

180.   Knowing

Birds know how to fly,
spheres cruise along their orbits,
sailing into peace.

181. *Rules*

All the rules of life,
motion, light, gravity, cells,
frame journeys in time.

182. *Pantocrator*

All things are governed
so we can orientate,
assured of purpose.

183. *Timing*

All time moves forward
and I move along with it,
swimming with the sea.

184. Something

Something to live for…
sparks my engine room's neurons,
geared for action.

185. Positioned

No stranger am I
in a garden with a sky
flowing like water.

186. Township nocturne

Burst pipes, rubble, trash,
a human melee fills streets:
life on a knife's edge.

187. *Pandemic gloom*

Hospitals are full,
joblessness rises steeply:
pray for its downfall.

188. *Mirrors*

Walk on any path,
it's a mirror of the stars:
a living order.

189. *In passing*

We're just passing through:
with small opportunities
to do something good.

190. *Inheriting the earth*

The humble birthed life:
blessed are blue-green algae
who breathed into air.

191. *Ancestors*

I heard ancestors
playing in the savannah,
hunting and laughing.

192. *Tortoise (i)*

Nudging through the field,
a tortoise nibbles petals:
breakfast after rains.

193. Tortoise (ii)

The little brown tank,
fuelled with life's flower power,
trundles over veld.

194. Tortoise (iii)

Shy of the stranger,
he peeks out of his front door,
then hobbles away.

195. Home from home

My home is Cape Town,
Table Mountain looking out
on seas of nations.

196.   *Rise of Africa*

The old continent,
on its strong, tectonic plate,
spawned our human throngs.

197.   *Cosmic togetherness*

The one way is good,
a highway from the gold stars
straight into my heart.

198.   *Blue*

Cosmic dot in space,
blue is for sky and oceans:
atmospheric Earth.

199. Facing home

My true North is God,
without directions I'm lost:
he can lead me home.

200. A brief reflection

My strong youth I lost,
its glow of vital promise…
leaving me wiser.

201. Pandemic masks

The woman's eyes smiled,
his eyes twinkled in return:
a brief connection.

202. Coconuts

God makes good products.
Take coconuts. Food. Drink. Oil.
Good for skin and brain!

203. The cat and the 7/8th Moon

I glanced at the Moon,
then saw a cat bound to me:
made one by the sky.

204. Imperfections

No angel am I,
nor Cape Town, nor my country:
my mountain like God...

205. Delicate

Consciousness awoke,
my heart was born delicate:
life's symbiosis.

206. Mercy

Human mercy is...
relative; God's is timeless:
trust in what abides.

207. Cosmic

The sunlit design
of the cosmos is benign:
like a work of art.

208. Centred

I focus on truth,
a love beyond distractions:
observed laws of life.

209. Trillions of little batteries

Mitochondria,
mothered into my body,
spark all energy.

210. Run

Run with your fire,
fly while you are still so strong;
may your youth be blessed.

211.   *The superorder*

Existence is ruled,
goodness established in air:
you can find your way.

212.   *Being found*

Once in Africa
God found me, giving new life.
Hope makes me happy.

213.   *Striving*

Let me ever strive,
healing my imperfections:
balm for wounds and scars.

214. A haiku made

Lines nailed in my head,
truths popping out in moments:
the form of essence.

215. Realisation

I know I must be
a high value producer:
consuming with care.

216. Framework

My life has a frame,
all the rules of existence:
I'm one with purpose.

217. Going

Each day is a step,
I'm on my way, just going:
not yet arriving.

218. On hate

Call truth by its name;
if hate, what hate crimes follow
in its deadly wake?

219. Magpies

In the old oak tree
they gather, hungry, cawing,
soon ready to swoop.

220. *The blasphemy of autocracy*

He declares himself
eternally innocent:
this is lawlessness.

221. *What Nietzsche said*

"God is dead," he said,
with a trick of rhetoric.
No! *Nietzsche* is dead.

222. *Good and bad*

In a no-good world,
I live for one true goodness:
receiving God's grace.

223. The big blow up

Let love blow us up,
and make us all new again,
born over, better.

224. Code of growth

Mitosis, cell growth,
life's secret machinery;
creation's software.

225. Whole earth

A blue and green world
filled with cells of energy
vibrating with life.

226. Pride

Hubris is silent:
an auto-immune disease
you don't know you have.

227. Core connection

Feeling satisfied
in your private, inner soul?
God connects your core.

228. New perspective

Prayer makes things more real,
bringing heaven close to Earth,
planting seeds of faith.

229. Negation

Negativity
can poison mind and spirit:
be grateful for Time.

230. Transformations

Turn anger to peace,
fear to faith and hate to love:
the soul's alchemy.

231. Javelin

Orange are the flames
of javelins of light in space:
fast flights of photons.

232. Peace and war

A peace pre-exists.
Why else is war paint needed?
Humans aren't hostiles.

233. Vessel

May God be my guide,
becoming a form of love,
a spirit vessel.

234. On a scale

Inside our big dome
life is small, like a genome:
cells of hope divide.

235. Anger

Faith fights fear, but...
what cures anger within,
but balm for its pain?

236. Coded

Switch your power on,
reboot software of your heart:
check for viruses.

237. Our clocks

Keep your clock ticking,
your scoreboard ticking over:
waste not your seconds.

238. *Knowledge*

Cells know what to do,
the cosmos knows how to think...
forming awareness.

239. *Wheels of justice*

The showman's boast ends,
the bully's story proves false:
the cheats hide away.

240. *Size of our dreams*

Our dreams are wider
than oceans, rivers, deserts
and all pettiness.

241.   No longer young

Okay, youth is gone,
time went by like a river
made fresh by full rains.

242.   Thanks, again

Thank you, my Father
for saving me so strongly
from such weaknesses.

243.   No panic

No need to panic,
the sunlight is straight and sure,
Earth's orbit secure.

244. Cleansed

Flush me clean of pain,
strengthen my integrity,
ready for today.

245. Nuances

Living is nuanced
like a spectrum of colour
hiding in plain sight.

246. A time and place for love

That was where our lives
intersected forever:
joined to a journey.

247. A small world

This is my small world
which God gave me to cherish,
to make me more whole.

248. Soul pledge

My soul is for right,
my heart is for life's goodness,
seeking God's high will.

249. Freshness

In freshness of rain,
or in clear morning light,
is the gentle touch.

250. Morning exercise

Prayer makes me stronger
for longer, to face the world,
my spirit bolder.

251. Micro-architectures

Double helixes,
the buckyball molecule:
small, mighty structures.

252. As I am

Love me as I am,
is all I ask of my life:
God exceeds my needs.

253. Core

Here's why I love God:
warm heart of the universe,
source of healing light.

254. Nocturne of Vangelis

If I could write words
as kind as these sublime notes,
they would bring tears.

255. Magnify my eyes

Bring my microscope
and my telescope to see
power and wonder.

256. Margin

Feeling free/unfree
rests on a margin's thin line:
we need to decide.

257. Multiply

Multiply the bread
and fishes for the masses,
food for the hungry.

258. Benediction

Multiply goodness,
blessed, beautiful Being,
bless us with goodness.

259. Cold front

A low-pressure zone
squeezes warmth from the Cape dome,
chilling flesh and bone.

260. Human future

Humankind we are,
men and women together,
birthing the future.

261. Half and half

Made from man-woman,
from mother and father flesh,
a bundle of genes.

262. Greenery

Drink the breath of trees.
Where would we be without plants?
On our way to Mars.

263. Fire

Life's like a fire,
full of flame and heat, then slows
to coals glowing late.

264. Coldness

Only in cold minds
is being emotional
some sort of big crime.

265. Mitochondriac

Hypochondriac?
Be a mitochondriac...
batteries of youth.

266. Wrong worship

Worship not phallus
nor skyscrapers nor money
nor roads to nowhere.

267. Walk

Walking with my wife
after work is done feels free,
our hearts hand in hand.

268. *Justice*

What you sow in words
you reap in thoughts and actions:
justice never sleeps.

269. *Hate-free*

Flush hate from my heart,
heal socio-phobia,
set love's power free.

270. *Trying again*

I tried to show love
but didn't do a good job.
Let me try again.

271. *Producers*

We are producers,
co-creating our home world;
dreams of woven silk.

272. *Ice cream man*

Cycling up the hill,
his bell jars my memory:
hot, childhood summers.

273. *Culture lockdown*

Fear's virus spreads,
theatres and movies shut,
until born again.

274. Return on Energy

Give me ROE.
Serene gratification:
children of gardens.

275. Post-Modernism

Nietzsche's negation
drives inversion of values:
upside-down thinking.

276. The surrendering

People cause anger
but it's a futile feeling,
achieving nothing.

277. *Musical moods*

There's Beethoven's Fifth,
and Stravinsky's Rite of Spring
then calm Clair de lune....

278. *Winter thought*

Bring spring sunshine soon
to warm up my blood and bones
and break buds in birth.

279. *Calling for change*

We need grace, not greed,
we need servants, not tyrants:
we need more healers.

280. Genome

Our own genome lives
as a unique stamp in cells
like seamless software.

281. These bright days

The days are longer,
the blue sky stronger, brighter:
summer soaks our world.

282. Violins

Violins are skin,
not rusty hinges creaking,
squeaking: but sighing.

283. Light touch

Play lightly on keys
not to be plinkety-plonk:
an angel's touch works.

284. My journey

Let not the show end,
even if heartaches happened:
the journey is all.

285. Aquatic

Cells live in water
in a water-based planet
swimming in wonder.

286. *Sweet air*

Plant roots suck water,
leaves strip dioxide from air:
seeping oxygen.

287. *Dead*

When I die, by grace....
a galaxy rider freed
at the speed of light.

288. *Form and function*

Think simplicity.
Purpose, function, ease of use:
manifest design.

289. Power

Power from above
gives insight to see the world
in the light of love.

290. Dreamy day

There were four seasons
in a day in the city:
my dreams like rainbows.

291. In all things

My living cells, like
matter in rocks, sand and ice,
serve laws of atoms.

292. *A word-picture of hate*

Hate is a mind cloud,
suffocating all vision,
darkening the heart.

293. *Provision*

Gently, it's raining,
forgiveness falls over me.
Daily bread is here.

294. *Magpie in the fir tree*

Magpie atop tree:
cold clouds roll in over him
as he stares below.

295. Solver

I'll be a solver,
with a toolbox of science
and a heart of faith.

296. One bleak night

Curfew: moonless streets,
air cold as a mortuary.
A lone watchdog barks.

297. Fertilise

Fertilising now,
under cold clouds, brings bright Spring:
future flowering.

298. Salt and pepper

In these lying times
the salt and pepper of truth
falls where it's sprinkled.

299. Lens of love

Let love be my lens
to see bigger and smaller,
to magnify God.

300. Repowered

Reboot my spirit,
believe stronger, love harder:
endlessly forgive.

301. Season of autocrats

Dripping with self-love,
the autocrats purr with pride,
playing tricks with truth.

302. Solitary peace

I love painless peace,
seeking out the Comforter,
praying to be healed.

303. Domination

Dominant fathers,
dominant mothers: bad news.
Gentle love wins wars.

304. Sunshine

My daily sun fix
is a vitamin D fill:
sunshine supplement.

305. Wherever

Whichever building,
whichever road, or country:
be with me, my God.

306. Sacred broth

Broth of sperm and eggs
births living humanity
through generations.

307. Recycled

I'm a recycler,
growing new cells from old ones,
rising new each day.

308. Ego talk

Egomaniacs.
Avoid them, don't pay them mind.
Humble your ego.

309. Think first

Slowly, calmly think.
Anger is no strategy.
Follow the high road.

310. *Real fantasies*

Basing fantasy
on reality sure beats
pure fantasy.

311. *Memes*

Thought climates evolve,
atmospheres of ideas,
spreading many memes.

312. *The Sun*

The Sun leaned over,
"What are you doing today?"
"Let me seek wisdom..."

---

313. Pandemic

The old world is gone,
in a year that never was.
What will awake next?

314. Death defined?

Death is like fainting,
with a teleportation
freely included.

315. Renewed

Trillions of cells
recycling and repairing:
always renewing.

316. Coldness

When cold grips your hands
warm them round a cup of tea:
dream of bluer skies.

317. Breath of life

Cells breathe energy
into the body's power:
nurture health with love.

318. 2020

It's the hardest time,
when your best isn't enough,
when the world turned bad.

319. Solar

Nature has systems,
like the home of our strong Sun
energising Earth.

320. Praise

Why is praise so scarce,
dead and buried like rare earths,
useless until held?

321. Becoming humane

From superficial
to fullest humanity:
switch your true love on.

322. Weaker

Though my eyes may fade
I can still see; though weaker,
my hope grows stronger.

323. Worrying

Through much, come worries,
while one purpose brings deep peace:
loving God and life.

324. A little life

Cell by cell, I grow,
and thought by thought, I ascend:
step by step, I go.

325. Benediction

Letting go, blesses,
giving up is no option:
seek your path to peace.

326. Guardians

No bosses in homes,
no bullies in the playground:
equal peace for all.

327. Infested

Poisonous mushrooms
of populism infest
fields of disrespect.

328. Above

This old world is hard,
but God remains good and kind,
above and beyond.

329. Sowing

Sow the love of God,
seeding peace, showing power,
healing hate and spite.

330. In praise of mitochondria

Little batteries
in trillions of my cells
breathing energy.

331. Turnings

Kaleidoscope twists:
a new moment: different.
Then it turns again.

332. A focus on facts, please

Show me all facts first,
since the truth can never be:
ideology.

333. Safe

In God's image made,
where else is safe, but in him
who wills to love us?

334. New path

My spade turned the soil;
as I laid a garden path,
I smelt the Earth breathe.

335. Ready

Made strong for today
by prayer, faith and grace: ready
for all new demands.

336. Sun cycle

The solar system
gives eternal energy
to creatures like me.

337. *Three principles*

Misrule breaks things up.
Give systems truth as ethos:
let love rule the world.

338. *Stronger*

Let love grow stronger,
let understanding increase
and truth be bolder.

339. *Sun*

Sun overhead burns,
like a hot oven; then dips:
potent orb of life.

340. Yellow

When I think of you,
I see bright Van Gogh yellow:
like glowing sunshine.

341. Blue

Birds love the blue orb
we live in, to fly inside:
breathing Earth's colour.

342. Red

Red is my heart's blood
that binds me to living air:
light of day and night.

343. Flight

It's the energy
wrapped in power-packed sunlight
that keeps me afloat.

344. Cat in sunlight

The cat shone in sun,
peach and grey coat, cool, green eyes
shining in her peace.

345. Rejected

Rejection creates
reservoirs of resentment,
ready to surface...

346. Miles Davis sound

Trumpet heaven flows
into me like soulful waves,
warm, yet super cool.

347. Dogmatic dangers

Ideology
is the passion of the times:
inciting hatred.

348. L'après-midi d'un faune

Like the *Rite of Spring*,
it's so new, its mystery
captures the senses.

349. *Politics of nostalgia*

'Rigid' turns 'frigid'
in political thinking
based on nostalgia.

350. *When?*

When will whites find it…
the image of God in blacks,
as if ever lost?

351. *The Spekboom*

Little carbon sponge,
Spekboom's good enough to eat:
strong and true are you.

352. *Word of welcome*

Hey, welcome, Summer,
you bring bright days and short nights,
heat beating strongly.

353. *Powered moments*

Standing in sunlight
revived me after illness:
power pouring in.

354. *Time picture*

Time, older than suns,
shines like summer days or nights,
free, like air, to use.

355. *The great sleep*

When I fall asleep,
I might wake up somewhere else:
a true UFO.

THE END

TITLES BY THE AUTHOR

SCIENCE FICTION

Chrysalis: A surgical sci-fi story about immortal potential

Earthrise 2036

DOCUMENTARY NOVEL

Heartbeat

POEMS

Three Hundred and Twenty-One Haiku

Not Yet in Heaven

Rebirths

PLAYS

The Archive - a play about the last days of Friedrich Nietzsche

NON-FICTION

Passage to Faith

A New Logic For Faith

The Courage to Believe

FUTURE STUDIES

Codebreaking our Future

Knowing our Future

www.beyondheads.com
www.michaeljlee.com
michael@positivedestiny.org

About the Author

Michael J. Lee, Master of Philosophy (Futures Studies) (cum laude), Master of Arts in English, Honours-Baccalaureus Theologiae (cum laude), Higher Education Diploma (with distinction).

Michael enjoys reading, writing, painting, sketching, jogging and watching powerful movies, having built up a private collection of several hundred DVDs and Blu-ray films spanning the entire history of cinema to the present. He has been married to Sannettha since 1990 and the couple have two daughters, Michaela, a food and cosmetic scientist, and Melissa, a linguist and business analyst.

Lee has been CEO of the ATM Industry Association (www.atmia. com), which has over 11,000 members in about 70 countries, since 2005. He is chairperson of the Consortium for Next Gen ATMs which has over 400 companies participating in this future-proofing exercise to link over 3 million ATMs with more than 5 billion mobile phones.

Michael is a qualified futurist, artist and writer living in Cape Town. In 2015, he published *Heartbeat,* a documentary novel about the world's first human heart transplant. His two works about understanding the social future through interdisciplinary causal analysis are *Knowing our Future* and *Codebreaking our Future,* both available on Amazon.com.

He has written two science fiction works, *Chrysalis,* a story about the world's first head transplant, and *Earthrise 2036,* a part-documentary, part-imaginary journey through the evolution of humanity from the rawest of origins in the Cradle of Humankind to the age of space exploration.

www.ingramcontent.com/pod-product-compliance
Lightning Source LLC
Chambersburg PA
CBHW022101050726